The Annotated Plutarch
ROMULUS

Plutarch's Lives Made Easy

with the

Annotated Plutarch Series

Original text by Plutarch
Annotated and Expanded by Rachel Lebowitz
Translation by George Long and Aubrey Stewart

Published by A Charlotte Mason Plenary, LLC

Published by A Charlotte Mason Plenary, LLC

The Annotated Plutarch
Romulus
Plutarch's Lives Made Easy
The Annotated Plutarch Series
Volume 4

Text by Plutarch and Rachel Lebowitz
Annotated and edited by Rachel Lebowitz
Translation by George Long and Aubrey Stewart

Issued in print and electronic formats.
ISBN: 978-1-954822-06-1 (paperback)

A Charlotte Mason Plenary is an educational company committed to furthering the ideas and educational philosophy of Charlotte Mason. We specialize in customizing curricula for families. We offer books, study guides, courses, and homeschooling consultations, including special needs consultations, based on the Charlotte Mason method of education.

Visit A Charlotte Mason Plenary at
CMPLENARY.COM

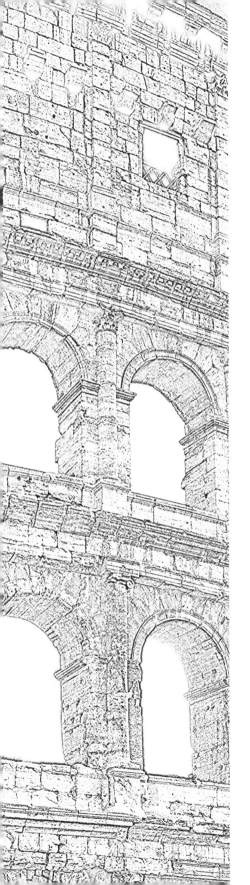

THE ANNOTATED PLUTARCH

ROMULUS

PLUTARCH'S LIVES MADE EASY
WITH THE
ANNOTATED PLUTARCH SERIES

TABLE OF CONTENTS

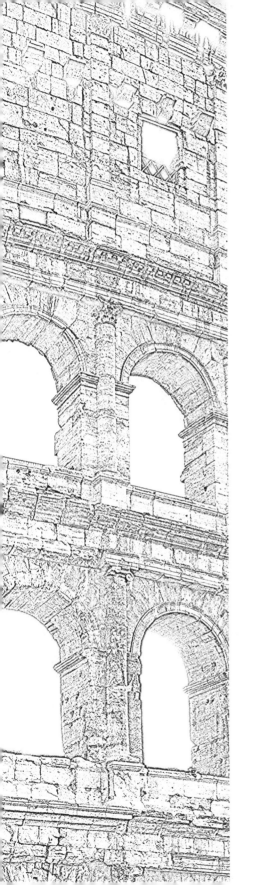

PREFACE

PREFACE
TO PLUTARCH'S LIVES

Plutarch just got a whole lot easier! And more fun too! Thank you for choosing The Annotated Plutarch Series from A Charlotte Mason Plenary.

HOW TO USE THE ANNOTATED PLUTARCH SERIES

This Annotated Plutarch Guide comes with the original text translated from the Greek. You do not need to purchase anything else to study Plutarch.

There are several sections I have written to help the student:

- The Introduction gives you biographical information about Plutarch himself.
- A "Who's Who" is included to help you understand the key players in this Guide.
- Lesson 1 sets the scene and will give you essential background information to begin your study.
- The last lesson wraps it up, connects the text to more modern events, and gives the student some important ideas to think about.

Other lessons include the original text by Plutarch. Just as Charlotte Mason used edited versions of Plutarch's *Lives* for her students, this text has been edited for content and length for your student. Anything unsuitable for students has been removed. You can feel comfortable about handing The Annotated Plutarch Series to your student for independent use.

For ease of reading, Plutarch's original text is in the inner column, and my added annotations are in the outer column. The annotations define vocabulary words and phrases and sometimes include pronunciations. The annotations also provide context to allow you to fully understand Plutarch's frequent references to the people, places, and culture of ancient Greece and Rome. **All annotated words are in bold type**. The goal is to highlight the text so that readers may gain a deeper understanding of it for themselves.

TRANSLATION

A Charlotte Mason Plenary uses the translation by George Long and Aubrey Stewart for most of The Annotated Plutarch Series. The Long translation is easier and more accessible for today's students, which will make the subject of Plutarch easier for you and your students.

We chose not to use the translation by Thomas North because it is a second translation of an earlier French translation done by Jacques Amyot in 1559. A translation of a translation is too far removed from the author's original words.

Long and Stewart translated Plutarch's *Lives* directly from Plutarch's original Greek. This makes the Long and Stewart translation more accurate.

George Long was a professor of Greek and Latin at University College in London. He was a major contributor to *Smith's Dictionary of Greek and Roman Antiquities*, and also wrote for the companion Biography edition. Aubrey Stewart was a Fellow at Trinity College in Cambridge, England. Together, they translated Plutarch's Lives from the original Greek into several English volumes in the 1800s.

PLUTARCH RESOURCES AND PICTURE STUDY

In addition, as you read through The Annotated Plutarch Series, you will find references to other resources that connect to Plutarch's story. These include classic paintings, poems, and other items that help further illustrate the text. It is my intent to provide you and your student with these additional resources to bring your Plutarch study to life.

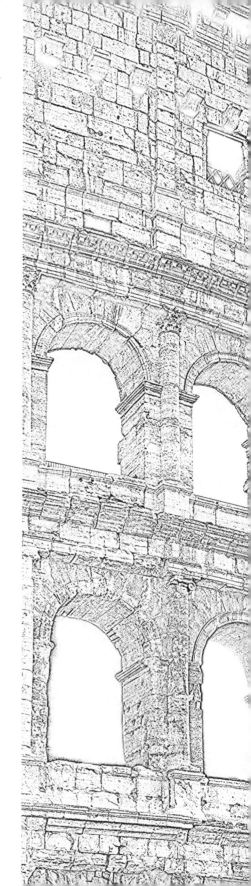

Some of the additional resources are free and can be found on the Plutarch Resources page of our website. I encourage you and your students to take advantage of these additional resources.

We also offer a Plutarch Picture Study for each life in The Annotated Plutarch Series. If you would like high-resolution images, printed copies of artwork, and additional background information, please visit our website to purchase the accompanying Plutarch Picture Study.

The Plutarch Picture Study helps students connect Plutarch's text to classical paintings and sculptures by famous artists. Artists across the ages have illustrated the fascinating stories found in Plutarch's *Lives.* The Picture Study also includes study questions about the text and the artwork to help students make a deeper connection.

For more information regarding the Resources Page and the Plutarch Picture Study, go to:

CMPLENARY.COM/PLUTARCH-RESOURCES

WHY STUDY PLUTARCH?

Plutarch was a Greek historian who lived c. 45-120 CE. He is known as the very first biographer. He wrote biographies of Greek and Roman men in his book *Lives of the Noble Greeks and Romans.* But he didn't just write about the accomplishments of these men, he also wrote about the smaller happenings of their lives in order to give us a glimpse into their character. This is why Charlotte Mason included Plutarch in her curriculum. It is about evaluating character.

What makes someone a great leader? What makes someone a tyrant? Plutarch shows us that it is the small decisions in a person's life that define his or her character. We then get to see the consequences of those decisions. Plutarch does not judge for us. He lays the man's life before us and we are left to judge. It is a truly remarkable way to study character and morality.

Charlotte's students started Citizenship Studies in Form 2B, or about 4th grade. The student spent a whole year reading *Stories from the History of Rome* by Beesly. This prepared the student for Plutarch by providing the context of Ancient Roman society. Then in Form 2A, or 5th grade, the student started reading one of Plutarch's *Lives* every term. This is the foundation of her character and citizenship teaching. It is not to be missed.

A THANK YOU

I hope The Annotated Plutarch Series makes Plutarch more accessible and more fun for you and your family. I sincerely hope you come to love Plutarch as much as I do!

Sincerely,

Rachel Lebowitz

A Charlotte Mason Plenary

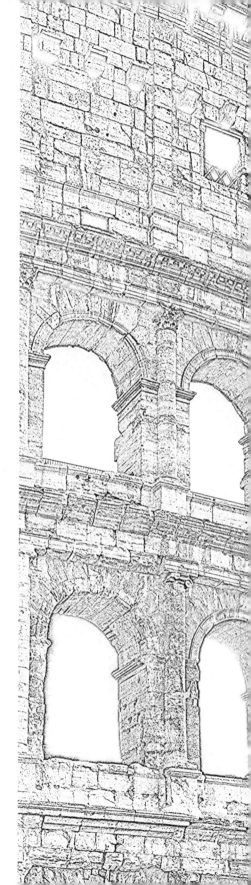

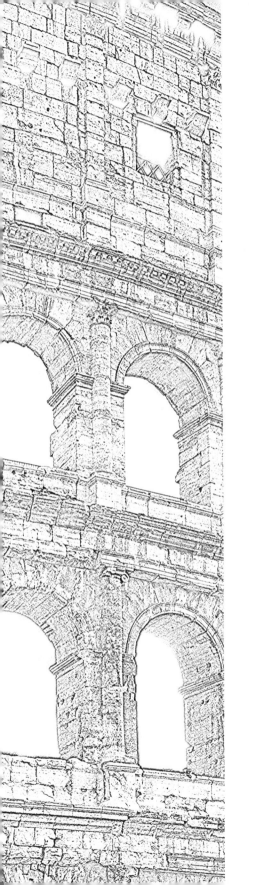

INTRODUCTION

Plenary Introduction
Who was Plutarch?

Plutarch, or Plutarkos in Greek, was an ancient Greek historian and philosopher. He is most well-known for his two works, *Parallel Lives* and *Moralia*. Plutarch lived in the little town of Chaeronea, Greece, from approximately 45-120 CE. His family appears to have been well-established there and his father was also an author and philosopher. From several passages in Plutarch's writings, we know that he studied at the Academy of Athens, which was founded by Plato.

Plutarch /ploo' tark/

But the most important event in his life was his journey to Rome. It was during this time that Plutarch officially became a Roman citizen and changed his name to **Lucius Mestrius Plutarchus**. During this trip, he did most of his research that would later become his book, *Lives of the Noble Greeks and Romans*, commonly known as *Parallel Lives*. Plutarch published the biographies in pairs, one Greek life with one Roman life, in an attempt to compare and contrast the two lives for their virtues and their failings. For example, the *Life of **Publicola***, a Roman Aristocrat, is paired with the *Life of Solon*, a Greek Athenian, both of whom were Statesmen.

Lucius Mestrius Plutarchus /loo'-shus mes'-tree-us ploo-tark'-us/

Publicola /pub-lǐ'-koh-luh/

Plutarch's *Lives* has been preserved through the centuries and has been translated from the original Greek into many other languages. The first translation from the original Greek was done in French by Jacques Amyot in 1559.

Just 20 years later, Thomas North published the first edition in English. North did not translate directly from the Greek, but instead used Amyot's French translation to publish his English translation in 1579. North's edition immediately became very popular in England during the reign of Queen Elizabeth I. Shakespeare used North's edition as source material for some of his historical plays, including *Julius Caesar*, *Antony and Cleopatra*, and *Coriolanus*, as well as references to Plutarch's *Life of Theseus* for *A Midsummer Night's Dream*.

Plutarch's influence spanned beyond England as well. People have always read Plutarch. His readers include George Washington, Thomas Jefferson, Alexander Hamilton, Benjamin Franklin, Abraham Lincoln, Ralph Waldo Emerson, and Theodore Roosevelt, just to name a few.

But why should *we* read Plutarch? What does the modern student gain from reading such an ancient text? What can we learn from a man who lived so long ago? Only a few of the men he wrote about are still known to us, such as Julius Caesar or Alexander the Great. Most of the names represented in Plutarch's *Lives* are completely unknown to the contemporary culture of today. Even Plutarch himself is not well-known except among scholars. So why read his stories?

Although Plutarch himself belongs to the ancients, his lessons are timeless. He was more concerned with documenting men's characters than their deeds, and *that* is what we have to learn from Plutarch: the value of discerning character.

Did You Know? Even fictional characters in literature have been known to read Plutarch! The monster in Mary Shelley's book, *Frankenstein*, finds a bag of books, one of which is Plutarch's *Lives of the Noble Greeks and Romans*. It is from this book that the monster learns about the idea of *character*.

Plutarch was quick to point out that he wrote *biographies*, not histories. In his *Life of Alexander*, Plutarch stated that a man's character is often revealed in subtle ways:

"a man's most brilliant actions prove nothing as to his true character, while some trifling incident, some casual remark or jest, will throw more light upon what manner of man he was than the bloodiest battle, the greatest array of armies, or the most important siege. Therefore, just as portrait painters pay most attention to those peculiarities of the face and eyes, in which the likeness consists, and care but little for the rest of the figure, so it is my duty to dwell especially upon those actions which reveal the workings of my heroes' minds, and from these to construct the portraits of their respective lives, leaving their battles and their great deeds to be recorded by others."

And it was in his intro to the *Life of **Timoleon*** that he wrote:

> *"It was for the sake of others that I first undertook to write biographies, but I soon began to dwell upon and delight in them for myself, endeavoring to the best of my ability to regulate my own life, and to make it like that of those who were reflected in their history as it were a mirror before me. By the study of their biographies, we receive each man as a guest into our minds, and we seem to understand their character as the result of personal acquaintance because we have obtained from their acts the best and most important means of forming an opinion about them. What greater pleasure could'st thou gain than this? What more valuable for the elevation of our own character?"*

Character—other people's and *our own*. That is what Plutarch urges us to consider.

Timoleon /tuh-moh'-lee-on/

Quotes are from *Plutarch's Lives: Translated from the Greek* by Aubrey Stewart, M.A., and George Long, M.A., Volume 1.

Who's Who

In Plutarch's Life of Romulus

PEOPLE

Aeneas .... Survivor of the Trojan War; nephew of King Priam of Troy; escaped Troy and traveled to Italy where he founded the city of Lavinium. His son, Ascanius (also known as Julius), founded the city of Alba Longa and was the city's first king.

Numitor .... Descendant of Aeneas; son of King Proca of Alba Longa; brother of Amulius; grandfather of Romulus and Remus

Amulius .... Descendant of Aeneas; son of King Proca of Alba Longa; brother of Numitor; usurped the throne from his brother Numitor to become King of Alba Longa; Great Uncle of Romulus and Remus

Rhea Silvia .... Daughter of Numitor; mother of Romulus and Remus

Antho .... Daughter of King Amulius; cousin to Rhea Silvia

Faustulus .... Swineherd of King Amulius; he and his wife rescued Romulus and Remus as infants and raised them as their own

Romulus .... Founder of Rome; twin brother to Remus

Remus .... Founder of Rome; twin brother to Romulus

Acron .... King of Caenina

Titus Tatius .... King of the Sabines

Tarpeia .... Woman who betrays the Roman army

Hersilia .... Wife of Romulus

Pythia .... The high priestess of the Temple of Apollo at Delphi. She was also known as the Oracle of Delphi and as the Pythoness.

Proculus .... A friend and companion of Romulus

PLACES

Latium .... A region in central western Italy in which the cities of Rome and Alba Longa were founded

Alba Longa .... A city in Latium which was founded by Aeneas; located about 12 miles southwest of Rome

Rome .... A city in Latium founded by Romulus and Remus which would later become the capital city of the Roman Empire

Gabii .... A city in Latium located about 11 miles east of Rome

Laurentum .... A city in Latium located about 16 miles southwest of Rome

Lavinium .... A city in Latium located about 3.5 miles south of Rome

Camerium .... A colony of Alba Longa

Etruria .... A region northwest of Rome in what is now modern-day Tuscany

Veii .... An ancient Etruscan city located about 10 miles northwest of Rome

Delphi .... Ancient Greek town on Mount Parnassus; it was the seat of the most important Greek temple and oracle of the Greek god Apollo, the Oracle of Delphi

GODS OF ANCIENT ROME

Vesta.............................. Goddess of the hearth, home, and family; her priestesses were the
Vestal Virgins

Asylaeus .... The patron god of vagabonds; the hill on which his temple was built
came to be called the Asylum

Consus .... The god of councils and secret conferences

Jupiter........................... The chief deity of the state religion of ancient Rome; Jupiter was the god
of the sky and thunder and is the equivalent of Zeus in ancient Greece

Juno .... Roman goddess who was the protector and special counselor of the state;
also known as Hera in Greek mythology

Ceres............................. Roman goddess of fertility and agriculture; her daughter was Proserpine;
also known as Demeter and Persephone in ancient Greece

Chthonic gods............... Greek deities associated with the underworld, including Hades,
Persephone, Demeter, and Hecate

Apollo .... Greek god who affords help and wards off evil; he was the patron deity
of Delphi and was believed to have spoken through the Oracle at Delphi

Vulcan........................... The Roman god of fire, including the fire of volcanoes, metalworking,
and the forge; his Greek counterpart is Hephaestus

Quirinus........................ One of the five major Roman gods; Quirinus, Jupiter, and Mars
constituted the trinity of the highest gods of the Roman state religion

LESSON 1
ROMULUS AND REMUS:
MEN OR MYTHS?

LESSON 1

ROMULUS AND REMUS: MEN OR MYTHS?

The founding of Rome is cloaked in mystery. It is a tangled web of legend, myth, and history: a king is usurped, a virgin priestess gives birth to twin boys, and a she-wolf suckles them.

Many details are clearly beyond belief, while a few circumstances have found a historical basis through archeological evidence.

True or not, the story has captured our imaginations for more than a millennia. What is it about the narrative of ancient Rome that fascinates us so?

Perhaps it is this tangled web that keeps us coming back for more. What part of the story is myth? What part is true? And can we ever hope to know the answers?

In Plutarch's *Life of Romulus*, we return to the scene of Rome's auspicious beginning with the story of Romulus and his twin brother Remus.

But the story of Rome actually begins half a century before Romulus and Remus are even born.

It begins in ancient Greece when a young Queen of Sparta falls in love with a Prince of Troy. Helen of Sparta is the most beautiful woman in the world. She is better known as **Helen of Troy**, the "face that launched a thousand ships."

When Helen leaves her husband, Menelaus, King of Sparta, for a handsome Prince of Troy named Paris, it sets off a chain of events that, ten years later, ends in the destruction of Troy.

The final year of the Trojan War is told in the *Iliad* by Homer. In this epic poem, we learn about Troy's King Priam and his family, his wife Hecuba, and some of their children.

In Greek mythology, **Helen** was said to be the most beautiful woman in the world. She was also the daughter of Zeus.

The quote "face that launched a thousand ships" refers to Helen and comes from the play *The Tragical History of Dr. Faustus* written in 1604 by Christopher Marlowe.

Hector, heir to the throne of Troy, was the bravest of warriors. But his little brother Paris was known more for his beauty than for his courage in battle. Their sisters included Cassandra and Creusa. Cassandra was a prophetess and foresaw the destruction of her home, but no one listened to her warnings.

Finally, we get to Creusa, who was married to Aeneas. And that's where the Trojan war connects with the founding of Rome and its hero, Romulus. Let us continue.

As Troy was burning, Creusa is killed, along with the royal family and most of the citizens of Troy. But Aeneas is destined by the gods to survive, and so, with the aid of the goddess Aphrodite, he escapes with his son, Ascanius, also known as Iulus or Julius.

What happens next is told in another epic poem, the *Aeneid* by Virgil.

Aeneas, after being commanded by the gods to flee, gathered a group of Troy's citizens, collectively known as the Aeneads, who then travel for years in search of a new home. They finally land on the west coast of present-day Italy where a king named Latinus ruled over Latium.

King Latinus welcomed Aeneas and the other Trojan refugees to Latium. The king's daughter, Lavinia, had been betrothed to a man named Turnus, king of a settlement to the south. But Latinus had a vision that Lavinia would marry Aeneas. Latinus heeded the prophecy and turned Turnus away. Turnus, however, declared war on Aeneas. Turnus was killed and Aeneas prevailed. Here, Virgil's account in the *Aeneid* ends.

But the legend continued. Aeneas married Lavinia and established the city of Lavinium in her honor.

Aeneas' son, Ascanius, founded a city called Alba Longa and is the first king of Alba Longa. From there, a long line of Aeneas' descendants ruled over Alba Longa.

Enter Proca, King of Alba Longa, and his two sons, Numitor and Amulius.

CMPLENARY.COM For more resources regarding this lesson, go to:
CMPLENARY.COM/PLUTARCH-RESOURCES/ROMULUS

DISCUSSION QUESTIONS

1. What about ancient Rome intrigues you? Why do you think that is?

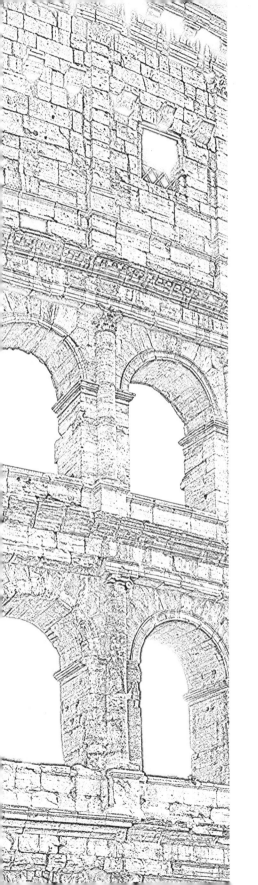

LESSON 2
THE SHE-WOLF

LESSON 2

THE SHE-WOLF

The dynasty established by Aeneas came down to two brothers, Numitor and Amulius.

Amulius offered his brother the choice between the sovereign power and the royal treasure, including the gold brought from Troy. Numitor chose the sovereign power. But Amulius, possessing all the treasure, and thereby having more power than his brother, easily dethroned him, and, as he feared his brother's daughter might have children who would avenge him, he made her a priestess of **Vesta**, sworn to celibacy forever. This lady was named Rhea Silvia.

After no long time, she was found to be with child, against the law of the Vestals. Her life was saved by the entreaties of Antho, Amulius' daughter, but Rhea Silva was imprisoned, that she might not be delivered without Amulius' knowledge.

She bore two children of remarkable beauty and size, and Amulius, all the more alarmed at this, bade an attendant take them and **expose** them.

Some say that this man's name was Faustulus, while others say that this was not his name, but that of their rescuer. However, he placed the infants in a cradle and went down to the river with the intention of throwing them into it, but seeing it running strong and turbulently, he feared to approach it, laid down the cradle near the bank, and went away. The river, which was in flood, rose, and gently floated off the cradle, and carried it down to a soft place.

It is said that while the infants were lying in this place, a she-wolf suckled them and that a woodpecker came and helped to feed and watch over them. These animals are sacred to the god Mars, and the Latins have a peculiar reverence and worship for the

Plutarch's text begins here. Lessons 2-10 include Plutarch's original text.

Vesta is the goddess of the hearth, home, and family in the religion of ancient Rome. Only her priestesses, the Vestal Virgins, were allowed in Vesta's temple where they tended the sacred fire.
There were six Vestal Virgins, chosen between the ages of 6 and 10, who then served as priestesses for 30 years.
If they broke their vow of chastity, they were sentenced to death by being buried alive.

Expose (verb) – to leave a child in the open to die from exposure to the elements

Gabii was an ancient city located about 15 miles north of Alba Longa.

Brigand (noun) — a member of a gang that ambushes and robs people in forests and mountains

CMPLENARY.COM For more resources regarding this lesson, go to:
CMPLENARY.COM/PLUTARCH-RESOURCES/ROMULUS

DISCUSSION QUESTIONS

1. Why do you think King Amulius spared the life Rhea Silvia?
2. What do you think about King Amulius' decision to expose the infants Romulus and Remus? Does it remind you of anything?
3. What do you think about the legend of the infants being sustained by a wolf and a woodpecker?
4. Discuss the artwork for this lesson as shown in *A Plutarch Picture Study: The Life of Romulus.*

woodpecker. These circumstances, therefore, seemed to confirm the tale of the mother of the children, that their father was the god Mars.

Now Faustulus, the swineherd of King Amulius, kept the children concealed from everyone, though some say that Numitor knew of it, and shared the expense of their education. They were sent to Gabii to learn their letters, and everything else that well-born children should know; and they were called Romulus and Remus because they were first seen suckling the wolf. Their noble birth showed itself while they were yet children, in their size and beauty; and when they grew up they were manly and high-spirited, of invincible courage and daring.

Romulus, however, was thought the wiser and more politic of the two, and in his discussions with the neighbors about pasture and hunting, gave them opportunities of noting that his disposition was one which led him to command rather than to obey.

On account of these qualities, the brothers were beloved by their equals and the poor, but they despised the king's officers and bailiffs and cared neither for their anger nor their threats. They led the lives and followed the pursuits of nobly born men, not valuing sloth and idleness, but exercise and hunting, defending the land against **brigands**, capturing plunderers, and avenging those who had suffered wrong. And thus they became famous.

LESSON 3
A SECRET REVEALED

LESSON 3

A SECRET REVEALED

Now a quarrel arose between the herdsmen of Numitor and those of Amulius, and cattle were driven off by the former. Amulius's men, enraged at this, fought and **routed** the others, and recovered a great part of the **booty**. They cared nothing for Numitor's anger, but collected together many needy persons and slaves, and filled them with a rebellious spirit.

While Romulus was absent at a sacrifice (for he was much addicted to sacrifices and **divination**), the herdsmen of Numitor fought with Remus, accompanied by a small band. After many wounds had been received on both sides, Numitor's men conquered and took Remus alive.

Remus was brought before Numitor, who did not punish him, as he feared Amulius's temper, but went to Amulius and begged for justice, saying that he had suffered wrong at the hands of Amulius's men.

All the people of Alba sympathized with Remus and feared that he would be unjustly put to death. Amulius, alarmed at them, handed over Remus to his brother Numitor, to deal with as he pleased.

Numitor took him, and as soon as he reached home, after admiring the bodily strength and stature of the youth, which surpassed all the rest, perceiving in his looks his courageous and fiery spirit, undismayed by his present circumstances, and having heard that his deeds corresponded to his appearance, and above all, as seems probable, some god being with him and watching over the first beginnings of great events, he was struck by the idea of asking him to tell the truth as to who he was, and how he was born, giving him confidence and encouragement by his kindly voice and looks.

Rout (verb) – to defeat and cause to retreat in disorder

Booty (noun) – valuable stolen goods, especially those seized in war

Divination (noun) – the practice of attempting to foretell future events by the interpretation of omens

Reminder: Numitor is not yet aware that Romulus and Remus are his grandsons.

The young man boldly said, "I will conceal nothing from you, for you seem more like a king than Amulius. You hear and judge before you punish, but he gives men up to be punished without a trial.

"Formerly we (for we are twins) understood that we were the sons of Faustulus and Laurentia, the king's servants; but now that we are brought before you as culprits, and are falsely accused and in danger of our lives, we have heard great things about ourselves. Whether they be true or not, we must now put them to the test.

"Our birth is said to be a secret, and our nursing and bringing up is yet stranger, for we were cast out to the beasts and the birds, and were fed by them, suckled by a she-wolf, and fed with morsels of food by a woodpecker as we lay in our cradle beside the great river.

"Our cradle still exists, carefully preserved, bound with brazen bands, on which is an indistinct inscription, which hereafter will serve as a means by which we may be recognized by our parents, but to no purpose if we are dead."

Numitor, considering the young man's story, and reckoning up the time from his apparent age, willingly embraced the hope which was dawning on his mind, and considered how he might obtain a secret interview with his daughter and tell her of all this; for she was still kept a close prisoner.

Faustulus, when he heard of Remus being captured and delivered up to Numitor, called upon Romulus to help him, and told him plainly all about his birth; although previously he had hinted so much, that anyone who paid attention to his words might have known nearly all about it; and he himself with the cradle ran to Numitor full of hopes and fears, now that matters had come to a critical point.

Faustulus was viewed with suspicion by the guards at the king's gate, and while they were treating him contemptuously, and confusing him by questions, they espied the cradle under his cloak.

Now it chanced that one of them had been one of those who had taken the children to cast them away and had been present when they were abandoned. This man, seeing the cradle and recognizing it by its make and the inscription on it, suspected the truth, and at once told King Amulius and brought Faustulus in to be examined.

Faustulus, in those dire straits, did not altogether remain unshaken, and yet did not quite allow his secret to be wrung from him. He admitted that the boys were alive, but said that they were living far away from Alba Longa and that he himself was bringing the cradle to Rhea Silvia, who had often longed to see and touch it to confirm her belief in the life of her children.

Now Amulius did what men generally do when excited by fear or rage. He sent, in a great hurry, one who was a good man and a friend of Numitor, bidding him to ask Numitor whether he had heard anything about the survival of the children. This man on arrival, finding Numitor all but embracing Remus, confirmed his belief that he was his grandson, and bade him take his measures quickly, remaining by him to offer his assistance.

Even had they wished it, there was no time for delay; for Romulus was already near, and no small number of the citizens, through hatred and fear of Amulius, were going out to join him.

Romulus himself brought no small force, arrayed in companies of a hundred each. Now as Remus raised a revolt within, while Romulus assailed the palace without, the despot Amulius was captured and put to death without having been able to do anything or take any measures for his own safety.

The greater part of the above story is doubted by many on account of its theatrical form, yet we ought not to disbelieve it when we consider what wondrous works are wrought by chance, and when, too, we reflect on the Roman Empire, which, had it not had a divine origin, never could have arrived at its present extent.

Reminder: Present day for Plutarch was more than two thousand years ago at the beginning of the Roman Empire.

CMPLENARY.COM For more resources regarding this lesson, go to:
CMPLENARY.COM/PLUTARCH-RESOURCES/ROMULUS

DISCUSSION QUESTIONS

1. Why do you think Remus decided to tell Numitor who he was?
2. What do you think of the character of Faustulus?
3. Why do you think the people rallied around Romulus and Remus?
4. Plutarch states that the Roman Empire's success is due to its divine origin. Do you agree or disagree?

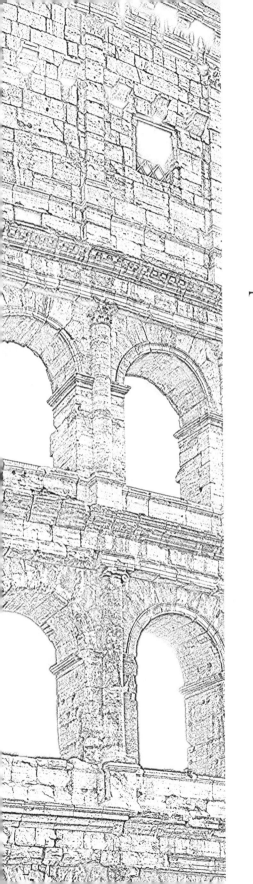

LESSON 4
THE FOUNDING OF ROME

LESSON 4

THE FOUNDING OF ROME

After the death of Amulius, and the reorganization of the kingdom, the twins, who would not live in Alba Longa as subjects, and did not wish to reign there during the life of their grandfather, Numitor, gave up the sovereign power to him.

Having made a suitable provision for their mother, they determined to dwell by themselves and to found a city in the parts in which they themselves had been reared.

It may also have been necessary, as many slaves and fugitives had gathered round them, either that they should disperse these men and so lose their entire power, or else go and dwell alone amongst them. It is clear, from the rape of the **Sabine women**, that the citizens of Alba Longa would not admit these outcasts into their own cities, since that deed was caused, not by **wanton insolence**, but by necessity, as they could not obtain wives by fair means; for after carrying the women off they treated them with the greatest respect.

Afterward, when the city was founded, they made it a sanctuary for people in distress to take refuge in, saying that it belonged to the god **Asylaeus**; and they received in it all sorts of persons, not giving up slaves to their masters, debtors to their creditors, or murderers to their judges, but saying that, in accordance with a **Pythian oracle**, the sanctuary was free to all; so that the city soon became full of men, for they say that at first, it contained no less than a thousand hearths.

When they were proceeding to found the city, they at once quarreled about its site. Romulus fixed upon a square piece of ground near **Palatine Hill** and wished the city to be built in that place, but Remus preferred a strong position on **Aventine Hill**.

Plutarch gives the account of Romulus' plan to abduct the **Sabine women** in the next lesson.

Wanton (adj) – deliberate and unprovoked violent action

Insolence (noun) – rude and disrespectful behavior

Asylaeus was the patron god of vagabonds. The hill on which his temple was built came to be called the Asylum. The word asylum means "to grant protection to someone who left their native country as a refugee."

In ancient Greece, the **Pythian Oracle** was the high priestess of the Temple of Apollo at Delphi. She was also known as the Oracle of Delphi and as the Pythoness.

Apollo was the god of prophecy and was seen as a source of guidance. As a result, the ancient Greeks built many sites for the oracles of Apollo. The Oracle of Delphi became the most well-known and influential of all the oracles. People would come from far and wide to consult the oracle at Delphi and meet with the Pythia.

Palatine Hill and **Aventine Hill** are two of the seven hills of Rome.

Augury is the practice of interpreting omens by watching the flight of birds. When the individual, known as the augur, interpreted these signs, it is referred to as "taking the auspices." The word auspices is Latin for "one who looks at birds." Depending upon how they were interpreted, the auspices from the gods could be favorable or unfavorable (auspicious or inauspicious).

They agreed to decide their dispute by **watching the flight of birds**, and having taken their seats apart, it is said that six vultures appeared to Remus, and afterward twice as many to Romulus. Some say that Remus really saw his vultures, but that Romulus only pretended to have seen them.

When Remus discovered the deceit, he was very angry, and while Romulus was digging a trench where the city wall was to be built, he jeered at the works and hindered them. At last, as he jumped over it, he was struck dead either by Romulus himself or by one of his companions.

Romulus, after burying Remus, consecrated his city, having fetched men who taught him how to perform the consecration according to sacred rites and ceremonies as though they were celebrating holy mysteries.

The **Comitium** was the original open-air public meeting space of Ancient Rome. It was the center of political activity.

A trench was dug in a circle round what is now the **Comitium**, and into it were flung first fruits of all those things which are honorable and necessary for men. Finally, each man brought a little of the earth of the country from which he came, flung it into one heap, and mixed it all together.

Next, they drew the outline of the city in the form of a circle, with this place as its center. And then Romulus, having fitted a plow with a brazen plowshare, and yoked to it a bull and a cow, himself plowed a deep furrow round the boundaries. It was the duty of his attendants to throw the clods inwards, which the plow turns up, and to let none of them fall outwards. By this line, they defined the extent of the fortifications, and it is called Pomoerium, which means "behind the walls" or "beyond the walls." Wherever they intended to place a gate, they took off the plowshare and carry the plow over, leaving a space. After this ceremony, they considered the entire wall sacred, except the gates; but if they were sacred also, they could not without scruple bring in and out necessaries and unclean things through them.

The Romans called the first day of each month the **calends**, signifying the start of a new lunar phase. The English word "calendar" is derived from this word. Modern calendars count the number of days after the first of each month; but the Roman calendar counted the number of days until certain upcoming dates, which is why Plutarch tells us the date is eleven days before the first of May.

It is agreed that the foundation of the city took place on the eleventh day before the **calends** of May (the 21st of April). And on this day the Romans keep a festival which they call the birthday of the city. At this feast, originally, we are told, they sacrificed nothing that has life but thought it right to keep the anniversary of the birth of the city pure and unpolluted by blood.

When the city was founded, Romulus first divided all the able-bodied males into regiments, each consisting of three thousand infantry and three hundred cavalry. These were named legions because they consisted of men of military age selected from the population. The rest of the people were now organized. They were called the Populus, and a hundred of the noblest were chosen from among them and formed into a council. These he called **Patricians**, and their assembly, the Senate.

The **Patricians** were the ruling class in ancient Rome.

This word Senate clearly means assembly of old men; and the members of it were named Patricians, according to some, because they were the fathers of legitimate offspring; according to others, because they were able to give an account of who their own fathers were, which few of the first colonists were able to do. Others say that it was from their *Patrocinium*, as they then called the patronage of their clients.

Patrocinium (noun) - patronage; the act of providing approval and support in return for protection and defense.

There is a legend that this word arose from one Patron, a companion of Evander, who was kind and helpful to his inferiors. But it is most reasonable to suppose that Romulus called them by this name because he intended the most powerful men to show kindness to their inferiors and to show the poorer classes that they ought not to fear the great nor grudge them their honors, but be on friendly terms with them, thinking of them and addressing them as fathers (Patres).

For, up to the present day, foreigners address the senators as Lords, but the Romans call them Conscript Fathers, using the most honorable and least offensive of their titles. Originally they were merely called the Fathers, but afterward, as more were enrolled, they were called Conscript Fathers. By this more dignified title, Romulus distinguished the Senate from the People; and he introduced another distinction between the powerful and

CMPLENARY.COM For more resources regarding this lesson,
go to:

CMPLENARY.COM/PLUTARCH-
RESOURCES/ROMULUS

DISCUSSION QUESTIONS

1. Why do you think Romulus killed Remus? Does this story remind you of anything?
2. Why do you think Romulus took such great lengths to consecrate the city and build a sacred wall around it?
3. Compare and contrast the scenes in which Romulus kills Remus and the sacrifices made during the celebration of the city's birthday.
4. Discuss the artwork for this lesson as shown in *A Plutarch Picture Study: The Life of Romulus*.

the common people by naming the former patrons, which means defenders, and the latter clients, which means dependants.

By this means, he implanted in them a mutual good feeling which was the source of great benefits, for the patrons acted as advocates for their clients in lawsuits, and in all cases became their advisers and friends. No law or magistrate could compel a patron to bear witness against his client, nor a client against his patron. Moreover, in later times, although all their other rights remained unimpaired, it was thought disgraceful for a patron to receive money from a client. So much for these matters.

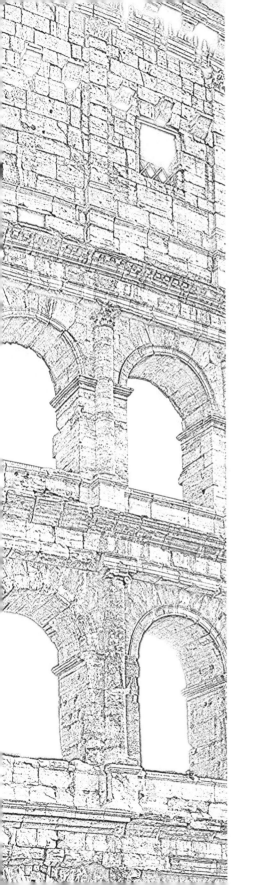

LESSON 5
THE ABDUCTION OF THE SABINE WOMEN

LESSON 5

THE ABDUCTION OF THE SABINE WOMEN

In the fourth month after the city was founded, we are told that the reckless deed of carrying off the Sabine women took place.

Some say that Romulus himself naturally loved war, and, being persuaded by some prophecies that Rome was fated to grow by wars and so reach the greatest prosperity, attacked the Sabines without provocation; and that he did not carry off many maidens, but only thirty, as though it was war that he desired more than wives for his followers. This is not probable.

Romulus saw that his city was newly filled with colonists, few of whom had wives, while most of them were a mixed multitude of poor or unknown origin, who were despised by the neighboring states, and expected by them shortly to fall to pieces. He intended his violence to lead to an alliance with the Sabines, as soon as the damsels became reconciled to their lot, and set about it as follows:

First, he circulated a rumor that the altar of some god had been discovered, hidden in the earth. This god was called **Consus**, either because he was the god of counsel (for the Romans to this day call their assembly *Concilium*, and their chief magistrates *consuls*, as it were those who take counsel on behalf of the people), or else it was the equestrian Neptune. The altar stands in the greater **hippodrome** and is kept concealed except during the horse races when it is uncovered. Some say that, as the whole plot was dark and mysterious, it was natural that the god's altar should be underground. When it was brought out, he proclaimed a splendid sacrifice in its honor, and games and shows open to all men.

Many people assembled to see these games, and Romulus sat among his nobles, dressed in a purple robe. The signal for the assault was that he should rise, unfold his cloak, and then again

In ancient Rome, **Consus** was the god of councils and was associated with secret conferences. His name is also related to the Concilium Plebis, or the Plebeian Council, which was the principal assembly of the common people of ancient Rome. His name is derived from the root condere (to store away) and he was also the god of grain storage. He had an altar at the southeast end of the racetrack in the Circus Maximus, the largest Roman hippodrome and one of the largest sports arenas ever built.

wrap it around him. Many men armed with swords stood around him, and at the signal, they drew their swords, rushed forward with a shout, and snatched up the daughters of the Sabines, but allowed the others to escape unharmed.

Some say that only thirty women were carried off, from whom the thirty tribes were named, but Valerius of Antium says five hundred and twenty-seven, and Juba says six hundred and eighty-three, all maidens.

This is the best **apology** for Romulus; for they only carried off one married woman, Hersilia, which proved that it was not through insolence or wickedness that they carried them off, but with the intention of forcibly effecting a union between the two races. Some say that Hersilia married Romulus himself and that he had children by her; one daughter, called Prima from her being the first-born, and one son, named Avillius.

When a treaty of peace was arranged between the Romans and the Sabines, a special provision was made about the women, that they were to do no work for the men except wool-spinning. And to the present day, the custom remains in force that the bride must not step over the threshold into her house, but be lifted over it and carried in, because the Sabine maidens were carried in forcibly, and did not walk in.

The rape of the Sabines took place upon the eighteenth day of the month Sextilis, which is now called August, on which day the feast of the Consualia is kept.

Apology (noun) – a reasoned argument in justification of something, typically a theory or religious doctrine

CMPLENARY.COM For more resources regarding this lesson, go to:
CMPLENARY.COM/PLUTARCH-RESOURCES/ROMULUS

DISCUSSION QUESTIONS
1. What is Plutarch's justification for the abduction of the Sabine women? Do you agree or disagree with Plutarch? Why or why not?
2. Why does Plutarch also call the abduction "reckless"?
3. In the last lesson, Plutarch said "after carrying the women off, they treated them with the greatest respect." What are your thoughts about this statement?
4. Can you think of any customs we have today that come from the story of the Sabine women?
5. Discuss the artwork for this lesson as shown in *A Plutarch Picture Study: The Life of Romulus.*

LESSON 6
WAR AND TREACHERY

LESSON 6

WAR AND TREACHERY

The Sabines were a numerous and warlike tribe, dwelling in unwalled villages, as though it was their birthright as a **Lacedaemonian** colony to be brave and fearless. Yet when they found themselves bound by such hostages to keep the peace, and in fear for their daughters, they sent an embassy to propose equitable and moderate terms, that Romulus should give back their daughters to them, and disavow the violence which had been used, and that afterward, the two nations should live together in amity and concord. But Romulus refused to deliver up the maidens and invited the Sabines to accept his alliance.

Lacedaemonian refers to Sparta, a prominent Greek city-state in Laconia. Spartans were one of the most feared and formidable military forces of ancient Greece.

While the other tribes were hesitating and considering what was to be done, **Acron**, the king of the Caenina, a man of spirit and renown in the wars, who had viewed Romulus with suspicion, now, after what he had done in carrying off the women, declared that Romulus was becoming dangerous, and would not be endurable unless he were chastised.

Acron was the king of Caenina, a city in Latium located near Rome, who declared war on Rome in response to the abduction of the Sabine women.

Acron at once began the war and marched with a great force, and Romulus marched to meet him. When they came in sight of each other they each challenged the other to fight, the soldiers on both sides looking on. Romulus made a vow that if he should overcome and kill his enemy he would himself carry his spoils to the temple of Jupiter and offer them to him. He overcame his adversary, slew him, routed his army, and captured his city.

He did not harm the inhabitants, except that he ordered them to demolish their houses and follow him to Rome to become citizens on equal terms with the rest. This is the policy by which Rome grew so great, namely that of absorbing conquered nations into herself on terms of equality.

Jupiter was the chief deity of the Roman state religion. He is the god of the sky and thunder. The Romans built the Temple of Jupiter Optimus Maximus to honor him. Jupiter is the equivalent of Zeus in ancient Greece.

A Roman **triumph** was a spectacular victory parade for a military commander who had won an important battle.

Dionysius of Halicarnassus was a Greek historian who wrote about Rome's founding in his book, *Roman Antiquities.*

Tarquin was the seventh (and last) King of Rome. He is commonly known as Tarquin the Proud because of his full name, Lucius Tarquinius Superbus. You can learn more about him in Plutarch's *Life of Publicola.*

Publicola, also known as Publius Valerius, was one of the leaders of the Roman revolution against King Tarquin in 509 BCE.

Fidenae, Crustumerium, and **Antemnae** were towns near Rome.

Garrison (noun) – a military post

Romulus, in order to make the fulfillment of his vow as pleasing to **Jupiter**, and as fine a spectacle for the citizens as he could, cut down a tall oak tree at his camp and fashioned it into a trophy, upon which he hung or fastened all the arms of Acron, each in its proper place. Then he girded on his own clothes, placed a crown of laurel upon his long hair, and, placing the trophy upright on his right shoulder, marched along in his armor, singing a song of victory, with all the army following him.

At Rome, the citizens received him with admiration and delight; and this procession was the origin of all the subsequent **triumphs** and the model which they imitated. **Dionysius** is in error when he says that Romulus used a chariot, for the historians tell us that **Tarquin** was the first of the kings who introduced this pomp into his triumphs. Others say that **Publicola** was the first to triumph in a chariot. The statues of Romulus bearing the trophy, which are to be seen in Rome, are all on foot.

After this, while the rest of the Sabines were still engaged in preparation for war, the inhabitants of **Fidenae, Crustumerium,** and **Antemnae** attacked the Romans. A battle took place in which they were all alike worsted, after which they permitted Romulus to take their cities, divide their lands, and incorporate them as citizens. Romulus divided all the lands among the citizens, except that which was held by the fathers of any of the maidens who had been carried off, which he allowed them to retain.

The remainder of the Sabines, angry at these successes, chose **Tatius** as their general and marched against Rome. The city was hard to attack, as the Capitol stood as an advanced fort to defend it. Here was placed a **garrison**, and Tarpeius was its commander, not the maiden Tarpeia, as some write. It was this Tarpeia, the daughter of the captain of the garrison, who betrayed the capital to the Sabines, for the sake of the golden bracelets which she saw them wearing. She asked as the price of her treachery that they should give her what they wore on their left arms. After making an agreement with Tatius, she opened a gate at night and let in the Sabines.

Now it appears that **Antigonus** was not singular when he said that he loved men when they were betraying, but hated them after they had betrayed; as also Caesar said, that he loved the treachery but hated the traitor; but this seems a common reflection about bad men by those who have need of them, just as we need the poison of certain venomous beasts; for they appreciate their value while they are making use of them, and loathe their wickedness when they have done with them.

And that was how Tarpeia was treated by Tatius. He ordered the Sabines to remember their agreement, and not to grudge her what was on their left arms. He himself first of all took off his gold armlet, and with it flung his great oblong shield. As all the rest did the like, she perished, being pelted with the gold bracelets and crushed by the number and weight of the shields.

Tarpeius also was convicted of treachery by Romulus, according to Juba.

However, as Tarpeia was buried there, the hill was called the Tarpeian hill until King Tarquinius, when he dedicated the place to Jupiter, removed her remains and abolished the name of Tarpeia. But even to this day, they call the rock in the Capitol the **Tarpeian Rock**, down which malefactors used to be flung.

Antigonus was a Greek General under Alexander the Great. His nickname was Monophthalmus, which means "one-eyed," because he lost an eye in battle. You can learn more about him in Plutarch's *Life of Eumenes*, another General who served under Alexander the Great.

The Tarpeian Rock is a steep cliff on the Capitoline Hill, which was used in Ancient Rome as a site of execution. Murderers, traitors, perjurors, and thieves were thrown off the cliff to their deaths. The cliff is about 80 feet high.

CMPLENARY.COM For more resources regarding this lesson, go to:
CMPLENARY.COM/PLUTARCH-RESOURCES/ROMULUS

DISCUSSION QUESTIONS

1. What do you think of King Acron's declaration regarding Romulus' actions and his subsequent decision to go to war with Rome?
2. What do you think the phrase "he loved the treachery but hated the traitor" means?
3. What do you think of Tarpeia's actions?
4. Discuss the artwork for this lesson as shown in *A Plutarch Picture Study: The Life of Romulus*.

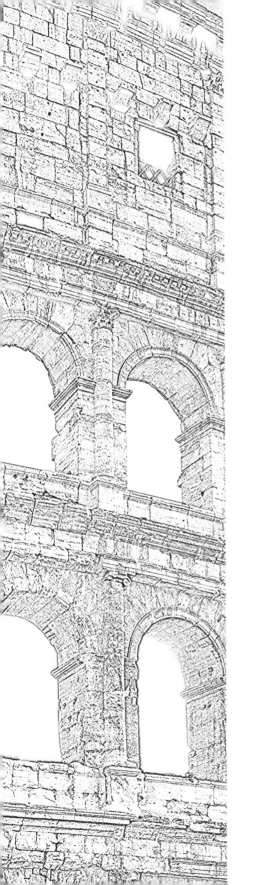

LESSON 7
THE INTERVENTION OF
THE SABINE WOMEN

LESSON 7

THE INTERVENTION OF
THE SABINE WOMEN

When the Sabines held the citadel, Romulus in fury challenged them to come down and fight. Tatius accepted his challenge with confidence, as he saw that, if overpowered, his men would have a strong place of refuge to retreat to. All the intermediate space, in which they were about to engage, was surrounded by hills, and so seemed to make a desperate battle necessary, as there were but narrow outlets for flight or pursuit.

It chanced, also, that the river had been in flood a few days before, and had left a deep muddy pool of water upon the level ground where the Forum now stands; so that men's footing was not certain, but difficult and treacherous. Here a piece of good fortune befell the Sabines as they heedlessly pressed forward.

Curtius, one of their chiefs, a man with a reputation for dashing courage, rode on horseback far before the rest. His horse plunged into this **morass**, and he, after trying to extricate him, at last finding it impossible, left him there and saved himself. This place, in memory of him, is still called the Gulf of Curtius.

Mettius Curtius was a Sabine warrior who fought under Titus Tatius. During a major battle, he narrowly escaped drowning in a swampy area.

Morass (noun) – a marsh or swamp

Warned of their danger, the Sabines fought a stout and indecisive battle in which many fell. Many combats took place in that narrow space, as we may suppose; and special mention is made of one, which proved the last, in which Romulus was struck on the head by a stone and like to fall, and unable to fight longer.

The Romans now gave way to the Sabines, and fled to the Palatine hill, abandoning the level ground. Romulus, now recovered from the blow, endeavored to stay his soldiers, and with loud shouts called upon them to stand firm and fight. But as the stream of soldiers poured on, and no one had the courage to face round, he lifted his hands to heaven and prayed to Jupiter to stay the army and not to allow the tottering state of Rome to fall, but to help it.

After his prayer, many were held back from flight by reverence for the king, and the fugitives suddenly resumed their confidence. They made their first stand where now is the temple of **Jupiter Stator**, which one may translate as "He who makes to stand firm." And then forming their ranks once more, they drove back the Sabines as far as what is now called the Palace, and the Temple of Vesta.

The temple of **Jupiter Stator** (Jupiter the Sustainer) was a sanctuary at the foot of the Palatine Hill in Rome. Romulus pledged to build it during the Battle of Lacus Curtius between the Roman army and the Sabines.

While they were preparing to fight as though the battle was only now just begun, they were restrained by a strange spectacle, beyond the power of words to express.

The daughters of the Sabines who had been carried off were seen rushing from all quarters, with loud shrieks and wailings, through the ranks and among the dead bodies, as though possessed by some god. Some of them carried infant children in their arms, and others wore their hair loose and disheveled. All of them kept addressing the Romans and the Sabines alternately by the most endearing names.

The hearts of both armies were melted, and they fell back so as to leave a space for the women between them. A murmur of sorrow ran through all the ranks, and a strong feeling of pity was excited by the sight of the women, and by their words, which began with arguments and upbraidings, but ended in entreaties and tears.

"What wrong have we done to you," said they, "that we should have suffered and should even now suffer such cruel treatment at your hands? We were violently and wrongfully torn away from our friends, and after we had been carried off we were neglected by our brothers, fathers, and relatives for so long a time, that now, bound by the closest of ties to our enemies, we tremble for our ravishers and wrongers when they fight, and weep when they fall. Ye would not come and tear us from our ravishers while we were yet maidens, but now ye would separate wives from their husbands, and mothers from their children, a worse piece of service to us than your former neglect.

"Even if it was not about us that you began to fight, you ought to cease now that you have become fathers-in-law, and grandfathers, and relatives of one another. But if the war is about us, then carry us off with your sons-in-law and our children, and give us our fathers and relatives, but do not take our husbands and children from us. We beseech you not to allow us to be carried off captive a second time."

Hersilia spoke at length in this fashion, and as the other women added their entreaties to hers, a truce was agreed upon, and the chiefs met in conference.

Hersilia is the Sabine wife of Romulus.

Hereupon the women made their husbands and children known to their fathers and brothers, fetched food and drink for such as needed it, and took the wounded into their own houses to be attended to there. Thus they let their friends see that they were mistresses of their own houses and that their husbands attended to their wishes and treated them with every respect.

CMPLENARY.COM For more resources regarding this lesson, go to:
CMPLENARY.COM/PLUTARCH-RESOURCES/ROMULUS

In the conference, it was accordingly determined that such women as chose to do so should continue to live with their husbands, free, as we have already related, from all work and duties except that of spinning wool; that the Romans and the Sabines should dwell together in the city, and that the city should be called Rome, after Romulus, and that they should both reign and command the army together.

DISCUSSION QUESTIONS
1. What are your thoughts on Hersilia's speech during the intervention of the Sabine women?
2. Discuss the artwork for this lesson as shown in *A Plutarch Picture Study: The Life of Romulus*.

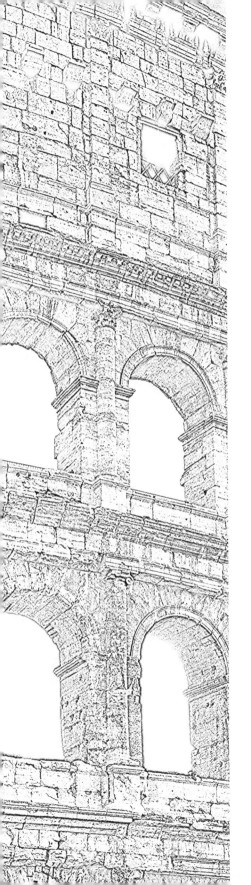

LESSON 8
THE ROMANS AND
SABINES MAKE PEACE

LESSON 8

THE ROMANS AND SABINES MAKE PEACE

Now that the city was doubled in numbers, a hundred more senators were elected from among the Sabines, and the legions were composed of six thousand infantry and six hundred cavalry. They also established three tribes, one for Romulus, another for Tatius, and a third for those who had asked for refuge and had been admitted as citizens.

Each tribe was divided into ten *centuries*, which some say were named after the women who were carried off; but this seems to be untrue, as many of them are named after places. However, many privileges were conferred upon the women, amongst which were that men should make way for them when they walked out, to say nothing disgraceful in their presence, or appear naked before them, on pain of being tried before the criminal court; and also that their children should wear the *bulla*, which is so called from its shape, which is like a bubble, and was worn round the neck, and also the broad purple border of their robe (*praetexta*).

The kings did not conduct their deliberations together, but each first took counsel with his own hundred senators, and then they all met together. Tatius dwelt where now is the temple of **Juno Moneta**, and Romulus by the steps of the Fair Shore, as it is called, which are at the descent from the Palatine hill into the great Circus.

Here they say the sacred cornel tree grew, the legend being that Romulus, to try his strength, threw a spear, with cornel-wood shaft, from Mount Aventine, and when the spear-head sunk into the ground, though many tried, no one was able to pull it out. The soil, which was fertile, suited the wood, and it budded and became the stem of a good-sized cornel tree.

Century (noun) – a grouping of 100.

The original 30 **Centuries** became the official legislative body of the Roman Republic. In the motto of ancient Rome, SPQR (Senatus Populusque Romanus), which means "The Senate and People of Rome," "people" refers to the citizens.

A **bulla** was an amulet that was given to male children. The amulet was worn around the neck to protect against evil spirits and forces.

A **toga praetexta** was a white robe with a purple border worn by a boy. When a boy turned 15, he then wore the toga virilis, the toga of manhood.

The Temple of **Juno Moneta** stood on Capitoline Hill overlooking the Roman Forum.
The goddess Juno was the protector and counselor of the state. With the epithet "Moneta," she became the protectress of the city's funds. Money was coined in her temple. The words "money" and "monetize" are from the Latin word "moneta."

After the death of Romulus, this was preserved and reverenced as one of the holiest objects in the city. A wall was built around it, and whenever anyone thought that it looked inclined to droop and wither he at once raised a shout to tell the bystanders, and they, just as if they were assisting to put out a fire, called for water, and came from all quarters carrying pots of water to the place. It is said that when Gaius Julius Caesar set out to repair the steps around it, and the workmen were digging near it, they unintentionally damaged the roots, and the tree died.

The Sabines adopted the Roman system of months. Romulus adopted the large oblong Sabine shield and gave up the round shields which he and the Romans had formerly carried. The two nations shared each other's festivals, not abolishing any which either had been wont to celebrate, but introducing several new ones, among which are the **Matronalia**, instituted in honor of the women at the end of the war.

The festival of the **Lupercalia** would seem, from the time of its celebration, to be a ceremony of purification; for it is held during the ominous days of February, a month whose name one might translate as "Purification"; and that particular day was originally called Febraté. The name of this feast in Greek signifies that of wolves, and it is thought, on this account, that the name may have arisen from the she-wolf, as we see that the **Luperci** start to run their course from the place where Romulus is said to have been exposed.

The circumstances of the ritual are such as to make it hard to conjecture their meaning. They slaughter goats, and then two youths of good family are brought to them. Then some with a bloody knife mark the foreheads of the youths, and others at once wipe the blood away with wool dipped in milk. The youths are expected to laugh when it is wiped away.

After this they cut the skins of the goats into strips and run about naked, except a girdle round the middle, striking with the thongs all whom they meet. Women in the prime of life do not

Matronalia was a festival celebrating women and motherhood. It commemorated the peace between the Romans and the Sabines as well as the dedication of a temple to Juno Lucina, the goddess of childbirth.

The festival of **Lupercalia** was a celebration of the Roman god Lupercus, also known as Pan or Faunus. The holiday was held in February and celebrated female fertility. It included a ritual foot race by the Lupercal priests known as **Luperci**.

Shakespeare's play, Julius Caesar, opens with the Lupercalia festival. Caesar's wife, Calpurnia, was unable to have children.

avoid being struck, as they believe that it assists them in childbirth and promotes fertility. It is also a peculiarity of this festival that the Luperci sacrifice a dog.

One **Butas** wrote on the origin of the Roman myths, saying that when Romulus and his party had killed Amulius, they ran back in their joy to the place where the she-wolf suckled them when little, and that the feast is typical of this, and that the young nobles run,

Butas was an ancient Greek poet who wrote an account of early Roman history, from which Plutarch quotes the origin of the Lupercalia.

> As, smiting all they met, that day
> from Alba, Romulus and Remus ran.

The bloody sword is placed upon their foreheads in token of the danger and slaughter of that day, and the wiping with the milk is in remembrance of their nurse. **Gaius Acilius** tells us that, before the foundation of Rome, the cattle of Romulus and Remus were missing, and they, after invoking Lupercus, ran out to search for them, naked, that they might not be inconvenienced by sweat; and that this is the reason that the Luperci ran about naked.

Gaius Acilius was a senator and historian of ancient Rome.

As for the dog, one would say that if the sacrifice is purificatory, it is sacrificed on behalf of those who use it. The Greeks, in their purificatory rites, sacrifice dogs and often make use of what is called **Periskylakismos**. But if this feast is in honor of the she-wolf, in gratitude for her suckling and preserving of Romulus, then it is very natural to sacrifice a dog, for it is an enemy of wolves; unless, indeed, the beast is put to death to punish it for hindering the Luperci when they ran their course.

Periskylakismos — sacrifices where puppies were killed and carried about.

CMPLENARY.COM For more resources regarding this lesson, go to: CMPLENARY.COM/PLUTARCH-RESOURCES/ROMULUS

DISCUSSION QUESTIONS
1. How did Romulus and Tatius organize the Roman government?
2. Describe the Lupercalia festival.

LESSON 9
A MURDER
AND A PLAGUE

LESSON 9

A MURDER AND A PLAGUE

It is said also that Romulus instituted the service of the sacred fire of Vestae, and the holy virgins who keep it lit, called Vestals. Others attribute this to Numa, though they say that Romulus was a very religious prince, and learned in **divination**, for which purpose he used to carry the crooked staff called *lituus*, with which to divide the heavens into spaces for the observation of the flight of birds.

Romulus also enacted some laws, the most arbitrary of which is that a wife cannot obtain a divorce from her husband, but that a husband may put away his wife for poisoning her children, counterfeiting keys, or adultery. If anyone put away his wife on other grounds than these, he enacted that half his property should go to his wife and half to the temple of **Ceres**. A man who divorced his wife was to make an offering to the **Chthonian gods**.

A peculiarity of his legislation is that, while he laid down no course of procedure in case of **parricide**, he speaks of all murder by the name of parricide, as though the one were an abominable, but the other an impossible crime. And for many years it appeared that he had rightly judged, for no one attempted anything of the kind at Rome for nearly six hundred years.

In the fifth year of the reign of Tatius, some of his relatives fell in with ambassadors from **Laurentum**, on their way to Rome, and endeavored to rob them. As the ambassadors would not submit to this but defended themselves, they slew them. Romulus at once gave it as his opinion that the authors of this great and audacious crime ought to be punished, but Tatius hushed the matter up and enabled them to escape. This is said to have been the only occasion upon which they were openly at variance, for in all other matters they acted with the greatest possible unanimity.

Divination (noun) – the practice of attempting to foretell future events by the interpretation of omens

The **lituus** was a crooked wand used by augurs to mark out a ritual space in the sky called a templum. The passage of birds through this space indicated divine favor or disfavor for a given undertaking.

Ceres, also known as Demeter, was the goddess of fertility and agriculture, the patron of farmers, and the protector of commoners. Her only daughter, Persephone, was kidnapped by the god of the underworld.

The **chthonic gods** were Greek deities associated with the underworld, including Hades, Persephone, Demeter, and Hecate, and they were all intertwined in the myth of the abduction of Persephone.

Parricide (noun) – the killing of a parent or other near relative

Laurentum was an ancient city of Latium, situated about 16 miles from Rome.

However, the relatives of the murdered men, as they were hindered by Tatius from receiving any justice, fell upon him when he and Romulus were offering sacrifice at Lavinium, and slew him, but respected Romulus, and praised him as a just man. He brought home the body of Tatius and buried it honorably.

But Romulus neglected altogether to exact any satisfaction for the murder. Some writers say that the city of **Lavinium**, in its terror, delivered up the murderers of Tatius, but that Romulus allowed them to depart, saying that blood had been atoned for by blood. This speech of his gave rise to some suspicion that he was not displeased at being rid of his colleague. However, it caused no disturbance in the state and did not move the Sabines to revolt, but partly out of regard for Romulus, fear of his power, and belief in his divine mission, they continued to live under his rule with cheerfulness and respect. Many foreign tribes also respected Romulus, and the more ancient Latin races sent him ambassadors and made treaties of friendship and alliance.

Lavinium was another city in ancient Latium. It was located about 3.5 miles south of Rome.

After this, a pestilence fell upon Rome, which slew men suddenly without previous sickness, and afflicted the crops and cattle with barrenness. A shower of blood also fell in the city, so that religious terror was added to the people's sufferings. As a similar visitation befell the citizens of Laurentum, it became evident that the wrath of the gods was visiting these cities because of the unavenged murders of Tatius and of the ambassadors. The guilty parties were delivered up on both sides, and duly punished, after which the plague was sensibly mitigated.

Lustration was a Roman purification ritual that included a procession and, in some circumstances, the sacrifice of a pig, a ram, and a bull.

The city of **Camerium** was a colony of Alba Longa and was established long before the founding of Rome.

Romulus also purified the city with **lustrations**, but before the plague ceased, the people of **Camerium** attacked the Romans, supposing that they would be unable to defend themselves on account of their misfortune, and overran their country. Nevertheless, Romulus instantly marched against them, slew six hundred of them in battle, and took their city. Half the survivors he transplanted to Rome, and settled twice as many Romans as the remainder at Camerium. So many citizens had he to spare after he had only inhabited Rome for about sixteen years. Among the other spoils, he carried off a brazen four-horse chariot from Camerium; this he dedicated in the temple of **Vulcan**, having placed in it a figure of himself being crowned by Victory.

As the city was now so flourishing, the weaker of the neighboring states made submission, and were glad to receive assurance that they would be unharmed; but the more powerful, fearing and envying Romulus, considered that they ought not to remain quiet, but ought to check the growth of Rome.

First the **Etruscans of Veii**, a people possessed of wide lands and a large city, began the war by demanding the surrender to them of Fidenae, which they claimed as belonging to them. This demand was not only unjust, but absurd, seeing that they had not assisted the people of Fidenae when they were fighting and in danger, but permitted them to be destroyed, and then demanded their houses and lands, when they were in the possession of others. Receiving a haughty answer from Romulus, they divided themselves into two bodies, with one of which they attacked Fidenae, and with the other went to meet Romulus.

At Fidenae they conquered the Romans, and slew two thousand; but they were defeated by Romulus, with a loss of eight thousand men. A second battle now took place at Fidenae, in which all agree that Romulus took the most important part, showing the greatest skill and courage, and a strength and swiftness more than mortal. But some accounts are altogether fabulous, such as that fourteen hundred were slain, more than half of whom Romulus slew with his own hand.

After the victory, Romulus did not pursue the beaten army, but marched straight to the city of Veii. The citizens, after so great a disaster, made no resistance, but at their own request were granted a treaty and alliance for a hundred years, gave up a large portion of their territory, their saltworks by the river, and handed over fifty of their leading men as hostages.

Vulcan is the god of fire, including the fire of volcanoes, metalworking, and the forge. He is often depicted with a blacksmith's hammer. The Vulcanalia was the annual festival held in his honor. His Greek counterpart is Hephaestus, the god of fire and smithery.

Veii was an important ancient Etruscan city situated less than 10 miles northwest of Rome in what is now modern-day Tuscany.

CMPLENARY.COM For more resources regarding this lesson, go to: CMPLENARY.COM/PLUTARCH-RESOURCES/ROMULUS

DISCUSSION QUESTIONS

1. What laws did Romulus enact? What do you think about the laws enacted?
2. How did the plague affect the city?
3. How did Romulus respond to the plague?
4. Discuss the artwork for this lesson as shown in *A Plutarch Picture Study: The Life of Romulus.*

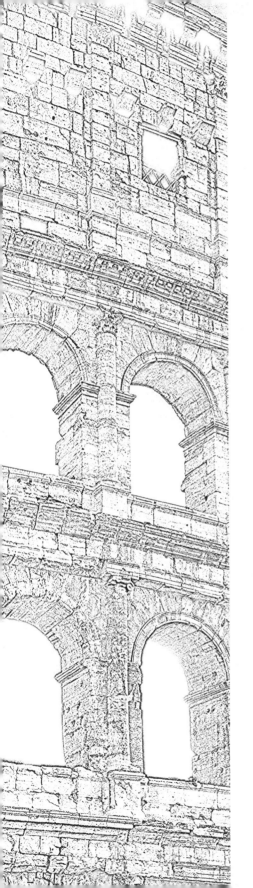

LESSON 10
ROMULUS QUIRINUS

LESSON 10

ROMULUS QUIRINUS

This was Romulus's last war. After it, he, like nearly all those who have risen to power and fame by a great and unexpected series of successes, became filled with self-confidence and arrogance, and, in place of his former popular manners, assumed the offensive style of a despot.

He wore a purple tunic, and a toga with a purple border, and did business reclining instead of sitting on a throne; and was always attended by the band of youths called **Celeres**, from their quickness in service.

Others, called **lictors**, walked before him with **staves** to keep off the crowd, and would bind anyone whom he might order into custody.

When Romulus' grandfather Numitor died in Alba, although he was evidently his heir, yet through a desire for popularity he left his claim unsettled and contented himself with appointing a chief magistrate for the people of Alba every year; thus teaching the Roman nobles to desire a freer constitution, which should not be so much encroached upon by the king.

For at Rome now even the so-called Fathers took no part in public affairs, but had merely their name and dignity, and were called into the Senate House more for form's sake than to express their opinions. When there, they listened in silence to Romulus's orders, and the only advantage which they possessed over the commons was that they knew the king's mind sooner than they did.

Worst of all was, that he of his own authority divided the land which was obtained in war amongst the soldiers, and restored the hostages to the Veientines, against the will of the Senate and without consulting it, by which he seemed purposely to insult it.

The **Celeres** were bodyguards to the first seven Kings of ancient Rome. They were the strongest and bravest warriors among the early Roman nobility and were the bravest and most loyal soldiers in the army.

A **lictor** was a Roman civil servant who acted as a bodyguard to the consul or other magistrate. They were also tasked with executing sentences of capital punishment. Romulus appointed 12 lictors to attend him.

Stave (noun) – a strong stick, especially one that is used as a weapon

In the Roman calendar system, the **Nones** fell on the first quarter moon of the month, about five to seven days after the new moon.

Scipio Africanus (236–184 BCE) was a Roman general responsible for Rome's victory against Carthage in the Second Punic War. He is regarded as one of the best military commanders and strategists of all time. His greatest military achievement was the defeat of Hannibal at the Battle of Zama in 202 BCE. This victory in Africa earned him the epithet Africanus. Scipio's death is said to have taken place under mysterious circumstances, as the cause is still unknown. We know that Plutarch wrote a *Life of Scipio*, but that manuscript no longer exists.

On this account, the Senate was suspected, when shortly after this Romulus miraculously disappeared. His disappearance took place on the **Nones** of the month now called July, but then Quintilis, leaving nothing certain or agreed on about his end except the date. Even now things happen in the same fashion as then; and we need not wonder at the uncertainty about the death of Romulus, when that of **Scipio Africanus**, in his own house after supper, proved so inexplicable, some saying that it arose from an evil habit of body, some that he had poisoned himself, some that his enemies had suffocated him during the night. And yet the corpse of Scipio lay openly exposed for all to see and gave all who saw it some ground for their conjectures; whereas Romulus suddenly disappeared, and no morsel of his body or shred of his garments were ever seen again.

Some supposed that the Senators fell upon Romulus in the Temple of Vulcan, and, after killing him, cut his body in pieces and each of them carried off one in the folds of his robe. Others think that his disappearance took place neither in the Temple of Vulcan, nor yet in the presence of the Senators alone, but say that Romulus was holding an assembly without the city, near a place called the Goat's Marsh, when suddenly strange and wonderful things took place in the heavens, and marvelous changes; for the sun's light was extinguished, and night fell, not calm and quiet, but with terrible thunderings, gusts of wind, and driving spray from all quarters. Hereupon the people took to flight in confusion, but the nobles collected together by themselves. When the storm was over, and the light returned, the people returned to the place again, and searched in vain for Romulus, but were told by the nobles not to trouble themselves to look for him, but to pray to Romulus and reverence him, for he had been caught up into heaven, and now would be a **propitious** god for them instead of a good king.

Propitious (adj) – indicating a good chance of success; favorable

The people believed this story and went their way rejoicing, and praying to him with good hope; but there were some who discussed the whole question in a harsh and unfriendly spirit, and blamed the nobles for encouraging the people to such acts of folly when they themselves were the murderers of the king.

Now **Julius Proculus**, one of the noblest patricians, and of good reputation, being one of the original colonists from Alba, and a friend and companion of Romulus, came into the Forum, and there upon his oath, and touching the most sacred things, stated before all men that as he was walking along the road, Romulus appeared, meeting him, more beautiful and taller than he had ever appeared before, with bright and glittering arms. Astonished at the vision, he had spoken thus:

> **Julius Proculus** is a figure in the legendary history of ancient Rome. His reported vision of Romulus shortly after his disappearance convinces the people of Rome to accept Romulus' divinity and the claims by the senate that he had been taken up by the gods in a whirlwind.

"O king, for what reason or with what object have you left us exposed to an unjust and hateful suspicion, and left the whole city desolate and plunged in the deepest grief?"

Romulus answered, "It pleased the gods, Proculus, that I should spend this much time among mankind, and after founding a city of the greatest power and glory should return to heaven whence I came. Fare thee well, and tell the Romans that by courage and self-control they will attain to the highest pitch of human power. I will ever be for you the kindly deity **Quirinus**."

> **Quirinus** was one of the five major Roman gods. Together with Jupiter and Mars, they constituted the trinity of the highest gods of the Roman state. Initially, he was the god of the Sabines and was identified with war. Plutarch tells the legend of how the Roman god Quirinus became associated with Romulus. The legend led to the formation of a new cult of Quirinus as the protector of Rome.

This tale was believed by the Romans from the manner of Proculus in relating it and from his oath, and indeed a religious feeling almost amounting to ecstasy seems to have taken hold of all present; for no one contradicted him, but all dismissed their suspicions entirely from their minds and prayed to Quirinus, worshiping him as a god.

This next account resembles the Greek legends of **Aristeas of Proconnesus**, and that of **Kleomedes of Astypalaea**. The story goes that Aristeas died in a fuller's shop and that when his friends came to fetch his body it had disappeared; then some persons who had just returned from travel said that they had met Aristeas walking along the road.

> **Aristeas** was a Greek poet and miracle worker. It was claimed that whenever he wished, his soul could leave his body and return again.

Kleomedes, we are told, was a man of unusual size and strength, but stupid and half-crazy, who did many deeds of violence, and at last, in a boy's school, struck, and broke in two, the column that

> **Kleomedes of Astypalaia** destroyed a school in a flash of insanity and killed all sixty children present. The citizens tried to stone him to death, but he hid in the temple of Athena and miraculously disappeared.

supported the roof, and brought it down. As the boys were killed, Kleomedes, pursued by the people, got into a wooden chest, and shut down the lid, holding it inside so that many men together were not able to force it open. They broke open the chest and found no man in it, dead or alive. Astonished at this, they sent an embassy to the oracle at Delphi, to whom the Pythia answered,

"Last of the heroes is Kleomedes of Astypalaea."

Alcmena is the mother of Heracles, whose father was the god Zeus. According to a Greek legend, when Alcmena died, she turned into a stone.

And it also related that the corpse of **Alcmena** when it was being carried out for burial, disappeared, and a stone was found lying on the bier in its place. And many such stories are told, in which, contrary to reason, the earthly parts of our bodies are described as being deified together with the spiritual parts. It is wicked and base to deny that virtue is a spiritual quality, but again it is foolish to mix earthly with heavenly things.

Pindar was an ancient Greek poet from Thebes.

We must admit, speaking with due caution, that, as **Pindar** has it, the bodies of all men follow overpowering Death, but there remains a living spirit, the image of eternity, for it alone comes from heaven. Thence it comes, and thither it returns again, not accompanied by the body, but only when it is most thoroughly separated and cleansed from it, and becomes pure and **incorporeal**.

Incorporeal (adj) – have no physical or material existence

Heraclitus of Ephesus was an ancient Greek philosopher.

This is the pure spirit which **Heraclitus** calls the best, which darts through the body like lightning through a cloud, whereas that which is clogged by the body is like a dull, cloudy exhalation, hard to free from the bonds of the body.

There is no reason, therefore, for supposing that the bodies of good men rise up into heaven, which is contrary to nature; but we must believe that men's virtues and their spirits most certainly, naturally, and rightly proceed from mankind to the heroes, and from them to demi-gods, and from thence, if they be raised above and purified from all mortal and earthly taint, even as is done in the holy mysteries, then, not by any empty vote of the senate, but in very truth and likelihood they are received among the gods, and meet with the most blessed and glorious end.

Some say that the name Quirinus, which Romulus received, means Mars; others that it was because his people were called Quirites. Others, again, say that the spear-head or spear was called by the ancients *Quiris*, and that the statue of Juno leaning on a spear is called Juno Quirites, and that the dart which is placed in the Regia is addressed as Mars, and that it is customary to present with a spear those who have distinguished themselves in war, and therefore that it was as a warrior, or god of war, that Romulus was called Quirinus.

A temple dedicated to him is built on the Quirinal Hill which bears his name, and the day of his translation is called the People's Flight, and the Nonæ Caprotinæ, because they go out of the city to the Goat's Marsh on that day to sacrifice.

Romulus is said to have been fifty-four years old, and to be in the thirty-eighth year of his reign when he disappeared from the world.

End of Plutarch's text

CMPLENARY.COM For more resources regarding this lesson, go to:
CMPLENARY.COM/PLUTARCH-RESOURCES/ROMULUS

DISCUSSION QUESTIONS
1. What do you think happened to Romulus?
2. What advice does Romulus give to the Romans (via Proculus)?
3. How does Plutarch describe the body versus the spirit or soul?
4. Discuss the artwork for this lesson as shown in *A Plutarch Picture Study: The Life of Romulus*.

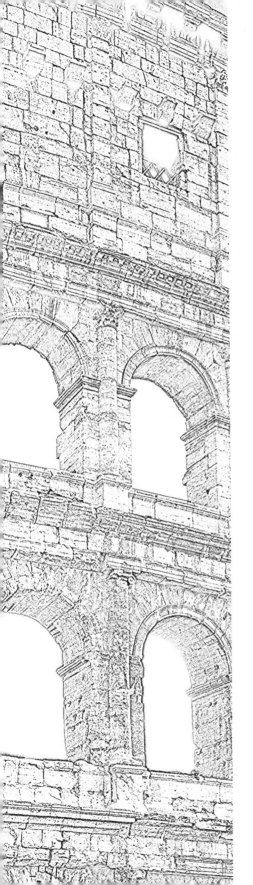

LESSON 11
ROMULUS:
ENDURING SYMBOL OF
ROMAN GREATNESS

LESSON 11

ROMULUS: ENDURING SYMBOL OF ROMAN GREATNESS

Romulus was the first of the seven kings of ancient Rome and ruled until 716 BCE. By the time of his death, the city of Rome had spread out from the Palatine to the Capitoline and then to the hills in the north. We now know that this small city would soon grow into an empire that would rule most of the ancient world.

The stirring tales of early Rome reveal so much about the Empire that it would later become.

Remember how Virgil's *Aeneid* traces Romulus' lineage back to Aeneas and the Trojan War? In that epic poem, he makes the claim that the son of Aeneas, Ascanius, was also known as Iulus or Julius.

Virgil lived during the reign of Rome's first emperor, Octavian, also known as Caesar Augustus. Octavian was the nephew of Julius Caesar. Both men were of the **Julian** line.

But before Augustus became emperor, Virgil had seen his country plagued by civil war, assassinations, and coups. After the assassination of Julius Caesar in 44 BCE, many men vied to take control of Rome and began warring against each other, including Octavian and Marc Antony. At the Battle of Actium in 31 BCE, Octavian defeated Antony and his ally Cleopatra of Egypt, consolidating power in himself alone.

Virgil was fortunate enough to enter the good graces of Augustus, and in time, the two men became friends. Augustus commissioned many works of poetry and literature from Virgil, including the *Aeneid*. In part, the *Aeneid* was commissioned to legitimize his reign and connect his family line to Aeneas and,

The **Julian** line, or gens Julia, was one of the most ancient patrician families of ancient Rome. Members of this family attained the highest dignities of the state and included Gaius Julius Caesar and the emperor Augustus.

more importantly, the gods. Augustus, with the help of Virgil, set out to claim that his reign was, in fact, ordained by the gods.

In her article, "Virgil as Propagandist," Mabel Gant Murphy writes:

"It is interesting in this age of propaganda to note that the force of this means of influencing public opinion was fully appreciated by Augustus Caesar, one of the most wily politicians of all times.

"Between 133 and 31 B.C., Italy had witnessed twelve civil wars and a long series of political murders. With the loss of civil control over the military forces, the commanders of the armies of Rome were successively masters of the city. Octavian was only the last victor in the long struggle.

"Men of Octavian's own time were very far from feeling that his victory was in itself an occasion for thanksgiving. Octavian fully appreciated this and realized the tremendous task which lay before him. If ever events called for effective propaganda to make the necessary mental adjustment between ruler and people, this was the time.

"Oratory and free speech had died with the Republic. Literature was the only means left for influencing public opinion. Augustus availed himself of it freely and collected about him a group of eminent writers. Publius Vergilius Maro (Virgil) became the poetic pillar of the reign. Aside from his great ability as a poet, Virgil was eminently fitted for the task. His high ideals and integrity were known to the people.

"He enjoyed the intimate friendship of the Emperor and wrote the Aeneid in honor of Augustus in order that he might celebrate in his poem the fame of Aeneas, from whose family Augustus desired to claim descent.

Suetonius was an ancient Roman historian. His most important work is a book called *The Twelve Caesars*, a set of biographies of twelve successive Roman rulers which begins with Julius Caesar and then includes biographies of the first eleven Emperors of the Roman Empire.

"**Suetonius** says that Augustus, while he was away on the Cantabrian expedition, wrote to the poet and urged that the first draft of the Aeneid, so far as it was completed, should be sent to him. When three books, the second, the fourth, and the sixth, were finally finished, Virgil read them to Augustus, [his wife, Livia, and his sister] Octavia; when Octavia heard the words, *Tu Marcellus eris*, she fainted [at the mention of her dead son, Marcellus]."

"The national idea of Rome was associated with belief in the divine origin of the city. The confidence of the Romans in themselves was intimately connected with their religious feelings and beliefs. Pride of birth and reverence for ancestors were very powerful and prevailing sentiments. Virgil appealed to such sentiments when in the Aeneid he not only recognized the descent of the Romans from Mars, but established their relation to 'Golden' **Venus** and thus traced their origin back to the King of Gods and Men.

"Virgil aimed to show that the great Empire which had had its beginnings in Aeneas and its culmination in Augustus was no mere work of human hands, but had been designed and built up in accordance with divine purpose. The passages [in the Aeneid] which indicate this are quite numerous. Jupiter, comforting Venus in her sorrow over the Trojan disaster, says:

> "The time shall come, as Rome's years roll on ... then shall be born the child of an illustrious line, one of thine own Trojans, Caesar, born to extend his empire to the ocean, his glory to the stars, -Julius, in name as in blood the heir of great Iulus. Him thou shalt one day welcome in safety to the sky, a warrior laden with Eastern spoils; to him, as to Aeneas, men shall pray and make their vows. In his days, war shall cease, and savage times grow mild. Faith with her hoary head, and Vesta, Quirinus, and Remus his brother, shall give law to the world." - *Aeneid*

Edith Hamilton, in her book *Mythology*, tells us that the *Aeneid* "was written when Augustus had taken over the bankrupt Roman world after the chaos that followed Julius Caesar's assassination. His strong hand ended the furious civil wars and brought about the **Pax Augusta.** Virgil and all his generation were fired with enthusiasm for the new order and the *Aeneid* was written to exalt the empire to provide a common national hero and a founder for the race destined to hold the world beneath its rule. Virgil's

Venus was the goddess of love, prosperity, and victory. Aeneas was the son of Venus and the Trojan prince Anchises. Via Romulus, son of Rhea Silvia and the god Mars, Rome connected it's origins to two of the most powerful Gods of the ancient pantheon: Mars (war) and Venus (love).

Pax Augusta, better known as the Pax Romana, means "The Peace of Augustus," or "The Peace of Rome." The phrase describes a 200-year-long time-span of peace and prosperity within Roman history that began with the reign of Caesar Augustus.

patriotic purpose is probably responsible for ... a hero for Rome that would make all other heroes seem insignificant."

That hero of Rome still stands, even today, as an ever-present symbol of Rome's greatness. Images of Romulus and Remus can be found throughout the world.

Historian Mary Beard, author of *SPQR: A History of Ancient Rome*, says:

"Even now, the image of a wolf suckling the baby Romulus and his twin brother Remus signals the origins of Rome. The famous bronze statue of the scene is one of the most copied and instantly recognizable works of Roman art, illustrated on thousands of souvenir postcards, tea towels, ashtrays, and fridge magnets, and plastered all over the modern city of the emblem of Roma football club.

"Because this image is so familiar, it is easy to take the story of Romulus and Remus – or Remus and Romulus, to give them their usual Roman order – rather too much for granted and to forget that it is one of the oddest historical legends of any city's foundation at any period, anywhere in the world. And myth or legend it certainly is, even though Romans assumed that it was, in broad terms, history. The wolf's nurturing of the twins is such a strange episode and a very peculiar tale that even ancient writers sometimes showed a healthy skepticism about the appearance of a conveniently lactating animal to suckle the pair of abandoned babies, right on cue. The rest of the narrative is an extraordinary mixture of puzzling details: not only the unusual idea of having two founders (Romulus *and* Remus) but also a series of decidedly unheroic elements from murder, to rape and abduction, to the bulk of Rome's first citizens being criminals and runaways.

"Whenever and wherever it originated, Roman writers never stopped telling, retelling, and intensely debating the story of Romulus and Remus ... To understand the ancient Romans, it is necessary to understand where they believed they came from and to think through the significance of the story of Romulus and Remus."

And so, whether it was propaganda, myth, history, or a combination of all three, the story of Romulus endures as a symbol of the greatness of Rome.

CMPLENARY.COM For more resources regarding this lesson, go to:

CMPLENARY.COM/PLUTARCH-RESOURCES/ROMULUS

Discussion Questions

1. What do you think about Romulus? Do you think he deserves hero status among Romans? Why or why not?
2. What was your favorite part of Plutarch's *Life of Romulus*?
3. What do you think of Virgil's *Aeneid* and how it might have been written as propaganda for Emperor Caesar Augustus?
4. Discuss the artwork for this lesson as shown in *A Plutarch Picture Study: The Life of Romulus*.

BIBLIOGRAPHY
PLUTARCH'S LIFE OF ROMULUS

Asimov, Isaac. *The Roman Republic*. Houghton Mifflin Co., 1966.

Beard, Mary. *SPQR: A History of Ancient Rome*. Liveright, 2016.

Bulfinch, Thomas. *Bulfinch's Mythology*. Grosset & Dunlap, 1883.

Hamilton, Edith. *Mythology*. Little, Brown and Co., 1942.

—. *The Roman Way*. W.W. Norton and Co., 1932.

Livy (Titus Livius). *The History of Rome*. Translated by William Roberts. J.M. Dent and Sons, 1921.

Malet, Albert. *The Ancient World*. Yesterday's Classics, 2021

Murphy, M.G. "Vergil as a Propagandist." The Classical Weekly 19, no. 21 (1926): 169–174.

Orlin, Eric M. *Temples, Religion, and Politics in the Roman Republic*. Brill, 2002.

Smith, William. *A Classical Dictionary of Biography, Mythology, and Geography*. John Murray, 1883.

—. *Dictionary of Greek and Roman Antiquities*. John Murray, 1859.

Stewart, Aubrey and George Long. *Plutarch's Lives Translated from the Greek in Four Volumes*. Bell and Sons, 1916.

OTHER RESOURCES BY A CHARLOTTE MASON PLENARY

THE ANNOTATED CHARLOTTE MASON SERIES

Home Education—Volume 1

Parents and Children—Volume 2

School Education—Volume 3

Ourselves—Volume 4

Formation of Character—Volume 5

A Philosophy of Education—Volume 6

Original Unabridged Text by Charlotte Mason

Annotated by Rachel Lebowitz

THE ANNOTATED PLUTARCH SERIES

The Annotated Plutarch–Publicola

The Annotated Plutarch–Pericles

The Annotated Plutarch–Julius Caesar

Original Text by Plutarch

Annotated and Expanded by Rachel Lebowitz

For a complete list of resources, or for more info about the Charlotte Mason method of education, please see A Charlotte Mason Plenary at:

CMPLENARY.COM

ABOUT THE AUTHOR

RACHEL LEBOWITZ is the owner of A Charlotte Mason Plenary, an author, a speaker, and a homeschooling mom.

She and her husband have always homeschooled their two children using the Charlotte Mason method of education. Rachel currently teaches Shakespeare and Plutarch at a local homeschool co-op and she leads a study group for parents who would like to learn more about implementing Charlotte Mason's methods. She has a Bachelor of Arts degree from the University of Houston where she studied Communications and Political Science. Before attending college, she traveled as a member of *Up With People*, a performing arts organization with a mission to transcend cultural barriers and create global understanding through music. After college, she spent many years as a Radio and Television Journalist. She currently lives in Texas with her husband, two children, two dogs, and one guinea pig.

You can find more information about the Charlotte Mason method at CMPLENARY.COM.

Made in the USA
Columbia, SC
10 January 2023

75824243R00052